A
FOUR-SEASON
GUIDE
— TO —
NORTH CAROLINA

Our State

EDITORS: Rachael Duane, Katie Saintsing
DESIGN DIRECTOR: Claudia Royston
DESIGNERS: Jason Chenier, Maggie Josey
FACT-CHECKER/PROOFREADER: Katie Fennell
INTERNS: Alexa Dysch, Rachel Glasser, Anjelique Kyriakos

CONTRIBUTORS: Troy Baker, Rosecrans Baldwin, Carson Blackwelder, Emily Burniston, Georgia Cassady, Jamie Chambliss, Matt Crossman, Mark Derewicz, Alex Dixon, Rachael Duane, Todd Dulaney, Alexa Dysch, Shannon Farlow, Katie Fennell, Chris Gigley, Rachel Glasser, Michael Graff, Leah Hughes, Susan Stafford Kelly, Anjelique Kyriakos, Caroline Leland, Ryan McGee, Kirstin Meyerhoeffer, Tripp Mickle, T. Edward Nickens, Chantel O'Neal, Katie Pegram, Sarah Perry, Taylor Rankin, Erin Reitz, Ali Rockett, Jeri Rowe, Katie Saintsing, Fred Sauceman, Julia Sayers, Lynn Setzer, Josh Shaffer, Susan Shinn, Brandon Sneed, Ryan Snyder, Mandy Stovall, Matt Tate, Jimmy Tomlin, Jeffrey Turner, Daniel Wallace, Chip Womick, Hope Yancey

A
FOUR-SEASON
GUIDE

—— TO ——

NORTH CAROLINA

Library of Congress Control Number: 2015907169

6
SPRING

28
SUMMER

Open your door to North Carolina's freshest season — a flower festival, a steeplechase, a round of golf at Pinehurst.

Rhododendron. Fireworks. Puppet shows. Boardwalks. Who doesn't love those lazy, hazy, crazy days of summer?

54
FALL

74
WINTER

Cravings for fair food and pumpkins and sweaters and bonfires remind us: Oh, how we've missed you, autumn.

Don't just endure winter. Embrace a town draped in lights, a freshly-cut Fraser fir, a cup of molten hot chocolate.

SPRING

Ask anyone in North Carolina what spring means, and you'll get as many answers as there are blooms on a dogwood tree. Perhaps the better question, instead, is what spring brings. Arriving along with petals and pollen, bees and birdsong, are steeplechases, flower festivals, and Easter. Parade down a street in your bonnet, or strap on a backpack for a hike. Whatever your newly minted pleasure, get out there: on a picnic, on a trail, in a cave, or at a craft beer bar. Open your door to North Carolina's freshest season.

From late March to early April, our state flower, the dogwood, appears in woods and on lawns from mountains to coast.

Multicolored wildflowers, cared for by the NCDOT, catch the eyes of North Carolina highway travelers.

FLOWER POWER

T ypically, little of beauty shows up on the side of the highway. But come spring, the North Carolina Department of Transportation's wildflower program, which began in 1985 as part of the state's highway beautification efforts, brings back-road scenery to our busiest highways.

The NCDOT keeps detailed records of plantings and blooming times, available at ncdot.org.

Here's where to spot our western wildflowers:

Buncombe County, Interstate 40 (Exit 37):
Mixed corn poppy, catchfly

Clay County, U.S. Highway 64:
Oxeye daisy, red corn poppy, catchfly

Haywood County, Interstate 40 (Exit 27):
Oxeye daisy, red corn poppy

Henderson County, Interstate 26:
Oxeye daisy, coreopsis

SPOT A WHITE SQUIRREL

At the first signs of warm weather, Brevard's unofficial mascot peeks out of its burrow. The white squirrel started appearing around town sometime in the 1950s, after H.H. Mull of Florida brought a pair of the pale critters to North Carolina to give to his niece, Barbara. Today, the squirrels abound in Toxaway, Cashiers, and Flat Rock, but they appear to prefer Brevard College, where they're fed by students and are used to admirers. Local artist Marcia Brennan was so inspired by the squirrels that she created a papier-mâché piece in their honor. Her work is on display at the Number 7 Arts Gallery, downtown.

BREVARD COLLEGE
1 Brevard College Drive
Brevard, NC 28712

Look for the white squirrel's distinctive head patches, dorsal stripes, and dark eyes, which distinguish this variety from albinos.

WAYNESVILLE RAMP FESTIVAL

Best known for its strong odor, the much-maligned ramp is enjoying an image makeover. Modern medical science has given credence to the Cherokee belief that this delectable wild mountain onion has therapeutic properties. Some say that if you eat a mess of ramps once a year, you'll live to see the next crop of ramps come in the following spring. New ramp leaves emerge in March or April, but they'll die back as the weather gets warmer — a brief, precious season celebrated every May at the Waynesville Ramp Festival.

For this year's festival information, visit downtownwaynesville.com.

Finding ramps often requires a rigorous hike. They're elevation-sensitive and thrive on the northern side of mountains, in cool, shady areas with damp soil.

DILLSBORO EASTER HAT PARADE

These are not ordinary hats. They're homemade, created with hot-glue guns and lots of imagination. Hats with chocolate bunnies, oversize stuffed chicks, and even real chicks in a birdcage. From near and far, paraders go to Dillsboro on the Saturday before Easter to march their hats two blocks around downtown — a kaleidoscope of creativity that's become one of the quirkiest holiday traditions in the state.

See more hats at visitdillsboro.org.

Lindsey Stack of Cullowhee lets her personality shine through a hat adorned with a dozen eggs and a dancing duck.

The interior of Linville Caverns continues to change as water slowly percolates down through Humpback Mountain.

LINVILLE CAVERNS

The outside world ends a few steps beyond the entrance to Linville Caverns. Water drip-drip-drips from the ceiling. The still air chills your skin, the temperature an ever-steady 52 degrees. Water and time have conspired to create stalagmites and stalactites that resemble everything from George Washington to a Franciscan monk marrying a kneeling bride and groom. These cool, dark recesses are also home to bats. But as tour guides assure visitors, they won't bother any casual explorers.

LINVILLE CAVERNS
19929 U.S. Highway 221 North
Marion, NC 28752
(828) 756-4171
linvillecaverns.com

EMILY CHAPLIN

In the towering branches of her birdhouse creations, Kinston designer Beth Greene puts her signature touch: an egg-filled bird's nest.

BIRDHOUSES ON PARADE, THE CAROLINA INN

When the colors of spring blossom and burst, these artful birdhouses add a whimsical touch to the classic elegance of the historic Carolina Inn in Chapel Hill.

The inn has been a gathering place in Chapel Hill since it opened in December 1924. The birdhouses scattered throughout set the perfect backdrop for spring-themed activities: lectures about horticulture and gardening, craft classes devoted to building birdhouses, Easter egg decorating for children, and one of the inn's defining traditions: afternoon tea. Sip floral teas with hints of jasmine or honeydew served in vintage china, while marveling at the birdhouses on parade.

THE CAROLINA INN
211 Pittsboro Street
Chapel Hill, NC 27516
(919) 933-2001
carolinainn.com

THE WATERWHEEL, OLD MILL OF GUILFORD

No matter how fast you drive down the hills of NC Highway 68 through Oak Ridge, it's hard to miss the giant red waterwheel that slowly spins in front of the Old Mill of Guilford. It's part of a gristmill on Beaver Creek that dates to 1767, before colonists declared their independence. In 1781, Lieutenant General Cornwallis seized the mill to grind grain for his soldiers.

Since then, the mill has had many different owners in its nearly two and a half centuries of operation. Each one has used the same traditional method of grinding grain with big, rough, rotating stones.

The current waterwheel is something fairly new — from around 1954. Stop in to buy all-natural, stone-ground cornmeal and grits for a perfect springtime brunch.

OLD MILL OF GUILFORD
1340 NC Highway 68
Oak Ridge, NC 27310
(336) 643-4783
oldmillofguilford.com

To reach the retail store, walk through the operating mill, where grain becomes flour and grits.

In addition to the
inn and restaurants,
Fearrington Village is
home to upscale shops.

GIFTS
FLOWERS
WEDDINGS

Bluebirds &
HOLLYH🌸CKS

URBAN ESCAPE IN FEARRINGTON VILLAGE

It's a unique getaway — a European-style hamlet set among forests and fields, and what once was 1,400 acres of farmland — only minutes from the Triangle's metropolitan hubbub. Beyond the metal silo, old milking barn, and fenced-in pastures, several specialty shops, a bookstore, restaurants, walking trails, and finely manicured gardens are spread under large oak trees.

The five-star Fearrington House restaurant is in the old Fearrington farmhouse, shaded by large oaks, and partially visible from U.S. Highway 15-501. Here, chefs use the best local produce and herbs, including some from Fearrington's own greenhouse and gardens.

Aside from several shops, the café, and The Granary restaurant, guests of the Fearrington House Inn have access to bikes and trails, bocce and tennis courts, a gym and two pools, a garden room with a fireplace and complimentary champagne and tea, all kinds of special events, and even a few waterfalls and lakes, at least one of which is good for fishing come spring.

Every one of the inn's 35 suites and rooms, as well as all of Fearrington, was designed with one thing in mind: to exceed expectations.

FEARRINGTON VILLAGE
2000 Fearrington Village Center
Pittsboro, NC 27312
(919) 542-4000
fearrington.com

CAMPBELL CREEK

Raven Rock State Park's marquee attraction, the Raven Rock, lures hundreds of people each year along its simple 2.6-mile jaunt at the onset of warm weather. For more walking and time in the forest, however, hike the Campbell Creek-Lanier Falls Loop, where early spring reveals the many holly trees that grow among the broadleaf trees. The absence of leaves also makes spotting mountain laurel easier; plus, you see more of the falls. Scan the fertile forest floor for spring wildflowers, Solomon's seal, and bloodroot. Wildlife also abounds here: Listen for woodpeckers, warblers, and wild turkeys.

RAVEN ROCK STATE PARK
3009 Raven Rock Road
Lillington, NC 27546

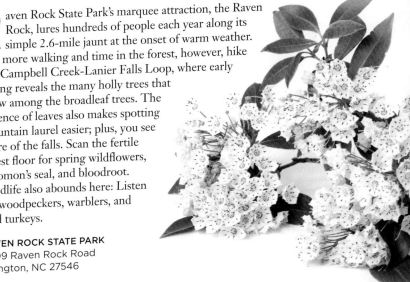

The Italianate-style Terrace Gardens (above) is the oldest part of the Sarah P. Duke Gardens — though not nearly as old as the elements of a traditional Japanese tea gathering (below), replicated at the arboretum.

PICNIC AT SARAH P. DUKE GARDENS

In the middle of Duke University's campus sits a 55-acre tract of horticulture heaven, recognized as one of the premier public gardens in the United States. The gardens are known for hosting Japanese tea gatherings in the Culberson Asiatic Arboretum's teahouse, where visitors are encouraged to focus on appreciating their surroundings and connecting authentically with the present moment. In other words, leave your preoccupations behind, and picnic in peace.

SARAH P. DUKE GARDENS
420 Anderson Street
Durham, NC 27708
(919) 684-3698
gardens.duke.edu

THE QUEEN'S CUP STEEPLECHASE

The Thoroughbreds won't start lining up until after noon, but the fun starts early as crowds roll in for one of the most Southern of our spring traditions: the steeplechase. The women wear sundresses and matching hats; the men wear polo shirts. They may come to Brookland-wood Racecourse in Mineral Springs for the horses, but the tailgating here is legendary. Bring out the mint juleps.

THE QUEEN'S CUP STEEPLECHASE
6103 Waxhaw Highway
Mineral Springs, NC 28108
(704) 843-7070
queenscup.org

At Brooklandwood Racecourse, a 300-acre farm south of Charlotte, the race is on for the prestigious Queen's Cup.

PINEHURST NO. 2

Sandy roads, like the ones that surround the 15th fairway, add to the rustic feel of Pinehurst No. 2. Rather than maintaining a dense rough, the groundskeepers of this legendary golf course have exposed the sand and wire grass that grow naturally, giving the course a distinctly Sandhills feel for the golfers — and tourist tagalongs — taking advantage of North Carolina's mild spring weather to spend a day at the links.

PINEHURST RESORT
80 Carolina Vista Drive
Pinehurst, NC 28374
(855) 235-8507
pinehurst.com

The home of American golf, Pinehurst No. 2 is notorious for its difficult greens. The best weapon for playing them? A good caddie.

WILMINGTON'S AZALEA FESTIVAL

Here they are, those funnel-shaped flowers that trumpet spring. Like Southerners, azaleas love sunshine, but they need a fair amount of shade to survive, which is one reason why they're a fixture in North Carolina neighborhoods. The annual NC Azalea Festival in Wilmington, held at the beginning of April, celebrates the flower with concerts, art shows, a street fair, and more.

NORTH CAROLINA AZALEA FESTIVAL
(910) 794-4650
ncazaleafestival.org

In the east, gardeners count on staple Southern Indica hybrid azaleas, which are on display during the festival's home-and-garden tours.

During the annual Daffodil Festival on the last
Saturday in March, Fremont's streets are paved in
gold and filled with entertainers, arts, and crafts.

FREMONT DAFFODIL FESTIVAL

Sometime after a newspaper
writer dubbed Fremont "The
Daffodil Town" in 1958,
residents decided to live up to their
reputation, holding the town's first
Daffodil Festival. Today, this festival
of yellow blooms remains Fremont's
signature kickoff to spring. Join the
town in celebrating with barbecue,
live music, and crafts.

FREMONT DAFFODIL FESTIVAL
(919) 242-5724
fremontdaffodilfestival.weebly.com

TAKE A COASTAL HIKE

With a beach vacation comes the luxury of being still. And for a few days, it's glorious. Then we start looking for something else: something to do. At this point (and especially in spring, when the weather isn't too hot), North Carolina affords a little-known beach indulgence called the coastal hike. High-marsh species collide with forest ecosystems, and visitors can enjoy a non-oceanic ecosystem that's nevertheless uniquely coastal.

1. Nags Head Woods Ecological Preserve, Nags Head

Five miles of trail on 1,111 acres. One of the largest remaining maritime forests along the East Coast. (252) 441-2525 or nature.org.

2. Carolina Beach State Park, Carolina Beach

Six miles along the Cape Fear River. Skirt a cypress pond and climb a 60-foot forested dune as you make your way past Venus flytraps and other carnivorous plants. (910) 458-8206 or ncparks.gov.

3. Neusiok Trail, Croatan National Forest, Havelock

Twenty miles. Not a short trail, but you can do a short hike. Best bet: Start at the northern trailhead in the Pine Cliff Picnic Area and walk along the Neuse River, through a pine savanna, and past colorful reminders of the region's human past. neusioktrail.org.

The Cedar Point Tideland Trail leads hikers into unexpected territory, where tidal marsh and hardwood forest merge.

4. Fort Fisher Hermit Trail, Fort Fisher State Recreation Area

This 2.2-mile out-and-back hike passes the concrete bunker that Robert E. Harrill, the Fort Fisher Hermit, called home for 16 years. (910) 458-5798 or greatoutdoorprovision.com.

5. Cedar Point Tideland Trail, Croatan National Forest

A 1.3-mile loop through tidal marshes. Start at the Cedar Point Campground, off NC Highway 58, about 1.5 miles north of the junction of NC highways 24 and 58. Open year-round. fs.usda.gov.

CRESWELL EASTER SUNRISE SERVICE

As members of Mount Hermon United Methodist, Cherry Church of God, St. John's Missionary Baptist, Mount Tabor Free Will Baptist, and Creswell Baptist begin to gather on the shore of Lake Phelps, it becomes apparent that this service is by no means conventional. "To me, when you're out there on the lake with the sun down and the moon high in the sky, it's about as close as you can get to God," the Rev. Eddie Coltrain once said. After gathering to celebrate rebirth through a sermon and singing, attendees make their way to Mount Hermon United Methodist to enjoy spicy sausage, scrambled eggs, and homemade biscuits.

PETTIGREW STATE PARK
2252 Lake Shore Road
Creswell, NC 27928

RAISE A GLASS TO NC BEER MONTH

North Carolina has more than 100 breweries and brewpubs to choose from — and the entire month of April to celebrate them.

WESTERN

A beer tour has to start somewhere, so why not Asheville? "Beer City USA," as it's come to be known, has more breweries per capita than any other U.S. city. Just to name a few...

Highland Brewing Company

Now the region's oldest operating beer maker, and one of the largest in the South, Highland Brewing Company takes the changing seasons very seriously. It unveils a special beer for each time of year and names it for a North Carolina peak.

HIGHLAND BREWING COMPANY
12 Old Charlotte Highway
Asheville, NC 28803
(828) 299-3370
highlandbrewing.com

Oyster House Brewing Company

Billy Klingel was first inspired to brew an oyster stout while working at Asheville's Lobster Trap restaurant, where seafood was plentiful. The resulting Moonstone Oyster Stout was such a success that Klingel built his own brewpub around it. What makes

the signature Moonstone Oyster Stout "unmatchable" is the high concentration of calcium carbonate, derived from boiling oyster shells in the brew.

OYSTER HOUSE BREWING COMPANY
625 Haywood Road
Asheville, NC 28806
(828) 575-9370
oysterhousebeers.com

Wicked Weed Brewing

Brothers Walt and Luke Dickinson have expanded their brewery with a tasting room and brewpub, and the Funkatorium, a barrel and sour brewery. Their West-Coast vision brought classics like big hoppy ales and authentic Belgian ales, as well as specialties including Asheville's first gluten-reduced beer and cocktail-inspired brews.

WICKED WEED BREWING
91 Biltmore Avenue
Asheville, NC 28801
(828) 575-9599
wickedweedbrewing.com

CENTRAL

Our best-stocked beer stores give us the freedom to pick and choose, taste and return, for that North Carolina brew we're loyal to, or something entirely new.

Carolina Beer Temple

Matthews's downtown beer store sells about 450 craft beers from around North Carolina and across the United States. Its bar has 16 rotating taps with a new beer menu printed daily. Plus, this temple even has its own throne: a tall red chair at the back of the store near the cooler.

CAROLINA BEER TEMPLE
131-1C Matthews Station Street
Matthews, NC 28105
(704) 847-2337
carolinabeertemple.net

Bestway Grocery

As people in Greensboro's tight-knit Lindley Park neighborhood step inside this grocery store, almost all of them share one thing in common: They start shopping on aisle 7, where Bestway Grocery's beer wall — which features at least 22 Tar Heel breweries — is located.

BESTWAY GROCERY
2113 Walker Avenue
Greensboro, NC 27403
(336) 272-4264

EASTERN

Putting the craft in craft beer, our eastern breweries pour a pint in style.

Weeping Radish

When the amendment passed in 1985 allowing beer to be sold in the same place that it was made, North Carolina got Weeping Radish, our state's first place to not just taste — but also see — good beer in the making. Since it first gave visitors a view with their brew, Weeping Radish has grown into a farm and butchery, as well.

WEEPING RADISH RESTAURANT AND BREWERY
6810 Caratoke Highway
Grandy, NC 27939
(252) 491-5205
weepingradish.com

Mother Earth Brewing

Local artist Dinah Sharpe Sylivant designs each label on Mother Earth's four signature beers to reflect the eastern region — like the Dark Cloud label, which depicts a storm cloud rolling over a tobacco farm. Or the label for Sisters of the Moon, conceived when cofounder Stephen Hill's three daughters began dancing around a campfire at his Kinston home.

MOTHER EARTH BREWING
311 North Herritage Street
Kinston, NC 28501
(252) 208-2437
motherearthbrewing.com

SUMMER

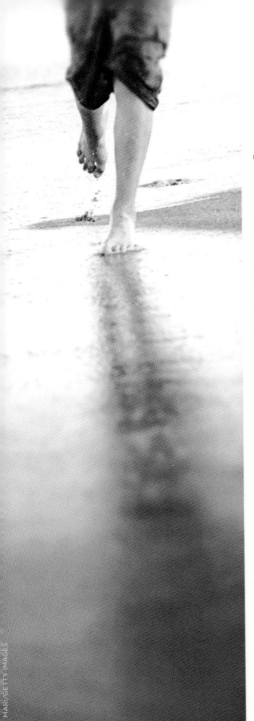

Tomato sandwiches and watermelon slices, magnolias and mowed lawns — the pleasures of a North Carolina summer are too myriad to mention. Tastes and aromas aside, there's something cooling, adventuresome, or relaxing for everyone in the Tar Heel State. Swimming holes and waterfalls tempt us, and we can find drama at retro drive-ins and contemporary theaters. Bare feet. Family vacations. Sunscreen. Steaks on a grill. Whirring fans. Who doesn't love, as the song goes, those lazy, hazy, crazy days of summer?

Summer at the Carolina coast: where sneak-attack splashes and rare sea treasures contain a delight that's ageless.

In western North Carolina, well-stocked waters (whose yield includes trout) and gorgeous settings are standard.

GONE FLY-FISHING

North Carolina has almost endless fly-fishing opportunities: Thousands of miles of trout-filled rivers, streams, and creeks flow across the western counties. Many are stocked by the North Carolina Wildlife Resources Commission, almost guaranteeing success every time you wade into the water. Others are more remote and challenge even the most experienced fisherman to snare the wild and wily trout.

1. **Tuckasegee River, Jackson County**
   Access: U.S. Highway 74 and
   NC Highway 107

2. **Wilson Creek, Caldwell County**
   Access: Wilson Creek Visitor Center
   7805 Brown Mountain Beach Road
   Collettsville, NC 28611
   (828) 759-0005
   friendsofwilsoncreek.org

3. **Watauga River, Watauga County**
   Access: NC Highway 194,
   Valle Crucis

4. **East Prong Roaring River,
   Wilkes County**
   Access: Stone Mountain State Park
   3042 Frank Parkway
   Roaring Gap, NC 28668
   (336) 957-8185

5. **Helton Creek, Ashe County**
   Access: NC Highway 16, just north
   of the New River

French Broad Rafting and Ziplines guides rookies down its namesake river.

RIDE THE RIVER RAPIDS

Whether you're looking to take on the Class IV rapids of the French Broad River, or working your tan from the back of a canoe, our state's river outfitters have plans in place for summer.

1. **French Broad Rafting
   and Ziplines, Marshall**
   Intricate routes through Class II, III, and IV rapids. Half- or full-day trips offered. Zip-line canopy tours and historic floats through Hot Springs also available.
   (800) 570-7238
   frenchbroadrafting.com

2. **Headwaters Outfitters, Rosman**
   Canoeing and kayaking through fast-moving currents. Guided fishing trips and overnight camping also available.
   (828) 877-3106
   headwatersoutfitters.com

GRANDFATHER MOUNTAIN HIGHLAND GAMES

As bagpipes and kettledrums resound in the distance, and red-, blue-, and yellow-striped canopies sprout in the meadow, Scots assemble in Linville for one of the largest gatherings of Scottish clans in the world. The games begin in MacRae Meadows with a torchlight ceremony known as the "raising of the clans." Then, for three days in July, participants challenge themselves in athletic and musical competitions. Numerous clan tents are set up to help guests trace their Scottish roots and learn more about their heritage.

GRANDFATHER MOUNTAIN HIGHLAND GAMES
(828) 733-1333
gmhg.org

WATERMELON WINE

Of the many delectable cold beverages to enjoy on a warm day, try a seasonal sweet wine from Lake James Cellars, named after nearby Lake James. These handcrafted wines are created from local North Carolina fruits, like watermelon and merlot grapes, which are blended to produce the cellars' seasonal wine specialty, "Summer Slice."

Available at local Glen Alpine stores and restaurants, or at the winery.

LAKE JAMES CELLARS
204 East Main Street
Glen Alpine, NC 28628
(828) 584-4551
lakejamescellars.com

The Grandfather Mountain Highland Games celebrates Scottish traditions like the weight-for-distance competition (left) and the "raising of the clans" (right).

The world's largest natural rhododendron garden grows at Roan Mountain, along the North Carolina-Tennessee border.

STOP TO SMELL THE RHODODENDRON

Explorers fell for it, enthusiasts still search for it, and communities rally around it. The rhododendron has been a feature of the Blue Ridge for centuries, and every summer, it covers our hillsides with color. Here's where to find it:

1. Chimney Rock State Park

Take a hike on the Great Woodland Adventure Trail or Four Seasons Trail on U.S. Highway 64/74 A.

2. Craggy Gardens
In mid-June, blooms cover these gardens, just 24 miles northeast of Asheville, at Blue Ridge Parkway Milepost 364.4.

3. Cherohala Skyway Drive
This road connecting Robbinsville to Tellico Plains, Tennessee, crosses through the Cherokee and Nantahala national forests. Blooms can be seen from the road during June and July.

4. Wayah Bald
Climb a 53-foot fire tower for the best view of the Nantahala National Forest, where native rhododendron bloom through June and early July.

5. Richland Balsam Overlook
Richland Balsam, at Milepost 431.4, is the highest point on the Blue Ridge Parkway. Catawba rhododendron covers the slope of this 6,410-foot-high peak.

Eighteenth-century attire and natural surroundings at *Horn in the West* take audience members back more than 200 years.

HORN IN THE WEST

The Daniel Boone Amphitheatre transports its audience to the rustic frontier, the setting for its annual production of *Horn in the West*. A sand-covered stage crunches under the actors' feet. The forests surrounding the amphitheatre play a constant chorus of crickets and owls that neither begins nor ends with the rising curtain or bowing cast. The nation's oldest Revolutionary War drama reminds audiences of the swelling pride with which their ancestors answered the "horn of freedom" — and makes a good case for spending a summer evening outdoors.

DANIEL BOONE AMPHITHEATRE
591 Horn in the West Drive
Boone, NC 28607
(828) 264-2120
horninthewest.com

BREVARD MUSIC CENTER FESTIVAL

What started as a band camp for boys in 1936 has evolved into a nonprofit educational institution that attracts internationally known musicians to Brevard for seven weeks every summer. The variety of genres is unrivaled: Choose from more than 80 performances of opera, choral, jazz, symphony, pops, and chamber music.

BREVARD MUSIC CENTER
(828) 862-2100
brevardmusic.org

RIDE THUNDER ROAD AT CAROWINDS

Which track do you choose: the blue track or the gray track? Is one really faster than the other? There's no wrong way to ride Thunder Road, but why not hop back in line and try the other track, too? Since first opening in 1976, the iconic coaster has seen countless riders whoop, holler, and raise their arms. But Carowinds isn't just for daredevils: It also offers rides, characters, and other experiences for those who prefer their fun at a slower pace.

CAROWINDS
14523 Carowinds Boulevard
Charlotte, NC 28273
(803) 548-5300
carowinds.com

Generations of thrill-seekers have grown up riding roller coasters at Carowinds. Thunder Road remains a Tar Heel favorite.

THE BULLHOLE, COOLEEMEE FALLS

At RiverPark in Woodleaf, you can hear the water as soon as you get out of the car. Regulars tote inner tubes along the trail to The Bullhole, a popular swimming spot and local hangout. At the swimming hole, a canopy of trees provides cool shade on hot summer days. Visitors catch a ride down the slippery brown slabs of giant rocks. The park also supplies a picnic shelter, restrooms, and three gravel walking paths.

RIVERPARK AT COOLEEMEE FALLS
645 Erwin Temple Church Road
Woodleaf, NC 27054
(336) 284-6040

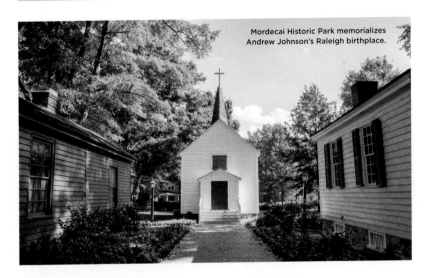
Mordecai Historic Park memorializes Andrew Johnson's Raleigh birthplace.

A PRESIDENTIAL DETOUR

During your summer travels, explore the birthplaces (yes, some are debated) of North Carolinians who have occupied the White House.

Andrew Jackson at the Museum of the Waxhaws
8215 Waxhaw Highway
Waxhaw, NC 28173
(704) 843-1832
museumofthewaxhaws.org

President James K. Polk State Historic Site
12031 Lancaster Highway
Pineville, NC 28134
(704) 889-7145
presjkpolk.com

Andrew Johnson at Mordecai Historic Park
1 Mimosa Street
Raleigh, NC 27604
raleighnc.gov/parks
(919) 857-4364

PAPERHAND PUPPET INTERVENTION

Paperhand Puppet Intervention is a whimsical way to spend a summer evening. But there's more to this program than entertainment. Putting on a show takes between 20 and 25 puppeteers and up to eight musicians. Not to mention the more than 100 volunteers who come to Paperhand's studio in Saxapahaw during the summer to help sew, construct, papier-mâché, and paint the puppets.

For more than 15 years, Paperhand Puppet Intervention has been creating and performing with giant puppets, although calling these awesome constructions "puppets" is a bit misleading. They are huge, and when they take the stage — walking, dancing, flying — it's like something from a dream.

For information on performances, visit paperhand.org.

In Saxapahaw, volunteers gather to turn odds and ends into giant puppets for Paperhand Puppet Intervention's shows.

SEE A DRIVE-IN MOVIE

The late 1950s and the early 1960s were the heyday of drive-in movie theaters. America's post-World War II love affair with the automobile was in full swing, and a pleasant summer night parked in front of an outdoor movie screen was a decidedly American pastime. In those days, North Carolina had more than 200 drive-in theaters.

But times changed and the drive-in theater slowly faded away. One by one, they locked their gates and darkened their screens. Those that still survive have two factors in common: a devoted core of regular patrons, and owners who love the business too much to let it die.

Most drive-ins focus on PG-rated movies, such as cartoons, superhero adventures, and science-fiction blockbusters. Admission prices are cheap, and on special summer nights, you can enjoy double features for the price of one admission.

1. **Albemarle: Badin Road Drive-In**
   2411 Badin Road
   (704) 983-2900
   badinroaddrivein.com

2. **Eden: Eden Drive-In**
   106 Fireman Club Road
   (336) 623-9669
   edendrivein.com

3. **Henderson: Raleigh Road Outdoor Theatre**
   3336 Raleigh Road
   (252) 438-6959
   raleighroaddrivein.com

When Tom English, director of the observatory, opens the Cline's dome doors during free public viewings, the telescope can be pointed in different directions, and the dome itself can spin 360 degrees.

STARGAZE AT CLINE OBSERVATORY

You've seen the moon before, but never quite like this. When you look through the eyepiece of the telescope at the Cline Observatory at Guilford Technical Community College in Jamestown, you can see the moon's surface in stunning detail: It doesn't look like cheese so much as marble, scarred by craters carved out by errant asteroids, comets, and early lunar volcanoes. Some of the craters are more than 1,000 miles across. Everyone who takes a turn at the telescope is in agreement: "Wow."

CLINE OBSERVATORY
601 East Main Street
Jamestown, NC 27282
(336) 334-4822
gtcc.edu/observatory

The Uwharrie Mountains Wine Trail comprises four wineries, including Dennis Vineyards in Albemarle.

THE UWHARRIE MOUNTAINS WINE TRAIL

There's no need to rush to the end of this trail, which begins in Salisbury, less than an hour northeast of Charlotte. The Uwharrie Mountains Wine Trail includes four wineries — Old Stone Winery, Uwharrie Vineyards, Dennis Vineyards, and Stony Mountain Vineyards — separated by less than 45 miles. Indulge in a day of touring and taste testing.

Visit uwharriemountainswinetrail.com for more trail information.

ROADSIDE TREAT

Summer vacations often include stops at roadside stands for an edible souvenir. David's Produce in Ellerbe is a favorite of those headed home after a weekend getaway at the beach. Travelers come for homegrown produce and a garden center full of flowering plants. Or for the neighboring ice cream shop, which serves sundaes, banana splits, and more. But rarely does a visitor leave without one of David's milkshakes, made with peaches plucked from the orchard right behind the stand.

DAVID'S PRODUCE
2932 U.S. Highway 220 North
Ellerbe, NC 28338
(910) 652-6413
Summer hours: Daily, 8 a.m.-5:30 p.m.

CANDOR PEACH FESTIVAL

In our state's peach capital, summer love takes the form of local, juicy, peachy goodness. The height of celebration for Candor's signature fruit occurs every July, as local peach growers take a day off from their posts at roadside stands to offer festivalgoers a basketful of fresh peaches, peach ice cream, and other delicious peach dishes.

CANDOR PEACH FESTIVAL
(910) 974-4221
townofcandornc.com

OCRAFOLK FESTIVAL

For the best seat in the house, look up. The people sitting in the oak tree branches above the Ocrafolk Festival's main stage are elevated into an overhead stream of salty breezes and guitar riffs. Here, the venue is as beloved as the music.

Music has been on the island for generations, Dave Tweedie says. These days, the main act on Ocracoke is Molasses Creek, of which Tweedie is an original member. The band plays host to the nearly 3,000 festivalgoers who come for Ocrafolk each June.

People come for the community. And when they come, they're not just observers, Tweedie says. "They're participants, as well."

Meaning the prime nook between two oak branches won't be occupied for long. It will soon be abandoned in favor of the swing dancing that has started up by the stage.

In Ocracoke, when the music starts, it's easy to get carried away.

OCRAFOLK FESTIVAL
(252) 921-0260
ocracokealive.com

The members of the band Molasses Creek are Ocrafolk veterans.

WE LOVE BEACH MUSIC

Beach music began as rhythm and blues that teenagers in North and South Carolina shagged to at the beach in the 1950s. Today, beach music still thrives in the Carolinas: Dozens of radio stations play it. Online streaming proliferates. There's no wrong way to love beach music, but learning to shag from one of our state's shag dancing clubs is a great place to start.

For shag dance locations, visit shagdance.com. For the basic steps, go to ourstate.com/videos/shagging.

Since the 1930s, the best view of Carolina Beach has been from the sky, on one of the boardwalk's 25 amusement rides.

CAROLINA BEACH BOARDWALK

A sk for a description of the Carolina Beach Boardwalk, and you'll hear words like "bright," "colorful," and "fun" — which could refer to any number of things: the pastel-colored buildings. The beach bands. The flashing carnival rides (all 25 of them are open every evening in the summer months).

All of these sights and sounds on the boardwalk welcome summer vacationers looking for a night out after a day at the beach. On Thursday nights — weather permitting — bands play into the night, and fireworks explode over the Atlantic Ocean. Or make plans to visit on a Tuesday — family night — when, for a low price, kids can ride as many carnival rides as they'd like (with parental permission).

And if your senses aren't heightened enough, head over to Britt's Donut Shop, where the homemade doughnuts are sure to send you soaring.

CAROLINA BEACH BOARDWALK
100 Cape Fear Boulevard
Carolina Beach, NC 28428
(813) 760-7678

Insider's peanut advice:
Stopping for the boiled variety?
Eat before you get back in your
car. Or else you may end up
with a lapful of salty juice.

PULL OVER FOR PEANUTS

Nothing is better than a salty cup full of fresh goobers. This down-home delicacy is easy to find on your way to the beach, at peanut stands like these:

1. Bertie County Peanuts

Bertie County Peanuts assures us that the shells of their raw peanuts are meant to look dark, mottled, even discolored — they're straight from the ground, unwashed and un-prettified.
217 U.S. Highway 13 North
Windsor, NC 27983
(800) 457-0005
pnuts.net

2. Houston's Peanuts

For anyone with a family reunion in their future — or a wedding, or a freezer full of Christmas presents — Houston's sells their "Raw Fancies and Jumbos" in a 100-pound burlap bag.
7329 Albert Street
Dublin, NC 28332
(910) 862-2136
houstonspeanuts.com

3. Sachs Peanuts

Sachs Peanuts began as a farm supply business in Clarkton. The owner, Edgar James Cox, sold "everything from mules to groceries." Today, the company sells only in-shell peanuts, with five offerings, from basic raw to Hot and Spicy with Tabasco.
9323 U.S. Highway 701 Business
Clarkton, NC 28433
(910) 647-4711
sachspeanuts.com

EAT A GOURMET S'MORE

This summer, if you're not comfortable with the grit and grime of camping, we know where you can find a tamer version of the classic campfire dessert in Atlantic Beach.

Amos Mosquito's, owned by Sandy and Hallock Howard and Dave Brumley, is a family restaurant that has been serving s'mores on its menu since it opened. Imagine watching a waiter approach your table carrying a small hibachi grill and six marshmallows ready to be skewered and toasted.

Now go, eat gourmet — and have your graham crackers, too.

AMOS MOSQUITO'S RESTAURANT & BAR
703 East Fort Macon Road
Atlantic Beach, NC 28512
(252) 247-6222

TAKE A LIGHTHOUSE PHOTO

Your guide to the seven historic lighthouses that stand on the Tar Heel shore starts with the venerable Old Baldy, built in 1817. The next oldest, Ocracoke Island Lighthouse, rises 76 feet above Silver Lake Harbor, while Cape Lookout Lighthouse soars 163 feet above wild dunes. Currituck Beach Lighthouse corkscrews up even higher: 214 steps to a panorama of Currituck Sound and Back Bay. Climb Oak Island Lighthouse, Cape Hatteras Lighthouse, and Bodie Island Lighthouse, and you can still imagine the old ways of utter dependance on a single beam of light.

While we may no longer rely solely on the guidance, certainty, and security of a fire on a hill, we still hunger for what those fires spoke of throughout the centuries: Here lies a wild shore, untamed and untrammeled, unknown and perilous — and eternally photogenic.

How can a single beacon represent so much? Our seven lighthouses powerfully reflect our own values — of innovation, endurance, and strength.

WILMINGTON'S SHAKESPEARE FESTIVAL

To see a Shakespeare play in London, England, in the 1600s, you paid a penny to go to the Globe Theatre. To see a Shakespeare play in Wilmington during the summer, it won't cost a cent. Cape Fear Shakespeare on the Green Festival began in 1993, when Dr. Stan Norman, a professor at the University of North Carolina Wilmington, wanted to give people the opportunity to attend a free Shakespeare festival. The tradition became the largest free Shakespeare festival in the Southeast; there's really no question of whether to be (there) or not to be.

GREENFIELD LAKE AMPHITHEATER
1941 Amphitheatre Drive
Wilmington, NC 28401
greenfieldlakeamphitheater.com

BEACH BALL

College baseball players from across the country come to the Coastal Plain League (CPL) for a taste of the big leagues. Founded in 1997, the CPL is regarded as one of the elite summer leagues in the country, including our very own Edenton Steamers, Wilmington Sharks, Wilson Tobs, Morehead City Marlins, and Fayetteville Swamp-Dogs. The league uses wooden bats to help prepare players for the pros, and major league teams have drafted more than 1,200 CPL alums. A 56-game schedule from late May to mid-August gives you plenty of time to see them play.

For game schedules, visit coastalplain.com.

A FIREWORKS-WORTHY FOURTH

The Fourth of July should ignite one's love of country, and three North Carolina celebrations do it best — with horseshoes flying, flags raised high, and theatrical declarations.

WESTERN

Fun and Games in Franklin

Along with traditional festivities like fair food and corn hole games, Franklin celebrates the Fourth of July with its famous horseshoe tournament, "The Plunger Toss." Though not necessarily patriotic, the competition provides daylong entertainment until the fireworks — one of the largest displays in western North Carolina — light up the night sky.

MACON COUNTY RECREATION PARK
1288 Georgia Road
Franklin, NC 28734
(828) 349-2090
franklinnc.com

CENTRAL

Fourth of July at the Capitol

The State Capitol has been home to our state's government for more than 170 years. In celebration of this legacy, an American flag is raised from a fire truck ladder between the building and Red Hat Amphitheater in Raleigh. Our capital's version of Independence Day includes food vendors, live music, and competitions like watermelon seed spitting, and ice cream and hot dog eating contests.

DOWNTOWN RALEIGH
500 Fayetteville Street
Raleigh, NC 27601
(919) 733-4994

EASTERN

New Bern

Fourth of July celebrations in New Bern have always been lively affairs: Throughout Tryon Palace's seven major buildings and 14 acres of gardens, visitors can enjoy concerts, crafts, theatrical performances, and demonstrations. But the major celebration starts when a dead ringer for William Hooper, one of the state's three signers of the Declaration, arrives at Tryon Palace by horse-drawn carriage, accompanied by an 18th-century fife and drum corps. He shushes the crowd and delivers a rousing rendition of the Declaration of Independence. But soon the audience steals the show, booing when they hear about how the king has done wrong.

TRYON PALACE
529 South Front Street
New Bern, NC 28562
(800) 767-1560
tryonpalace.org

FALL

You can feel it, sense it. The air grows crisper, the light clearer. You develop this craving for apples, and the urge to plop a pumpkin on your porch long before October 31. Dogwoods turn a burnished red, and sugar maples seem to be ablaze. And then there's that first fire on the first chilly night. The season's first sweater. The season's first stew. Hello, autumn. We'd forgotten how much we missed you.

Off of the Blue Ridge Parkway, near Blowing Rock, hikers get a glimpse of western North Carolina's famous fall hues, reflected in Price Lake.

APPLE PICKING

We learn to love apples at an early age: Granny Smiths, sliced and slathered in peanut butter. Galas, tucked into our lunch boxes. These are the year-round grocery store-friendly offerings we know well, but there's a world of fall-only fruit, too. This year, discover the heirloom apples our ancestors ate — Rome Beauty, Stayman's Winesap, Arkansas Black — at roadside stands, like Hendersonville's Mountain Fresh Orchards.

MOUNTAIN FRESH ORCHARDS
2887 Chimney Rock Road
Hendersonville, NC 28792
(828) 685-7606
mtnfreshorchards.com

APPLE SIPPING

Fermented apple juice, or hard cider, was one of the country's most prevalent drinks until the mid-20th century. As Prohibition took hold, the beverage's production declined. But thanks to pockets of producers, like McRitchie Winery and Ciderworks in Thurmond, cider is enjoying a renaissance. McRitchie cider is a blend of apple varieties from the last year's crop, mostly supplied from the Brushy Mountain region. As the juice goes through the pressurized tanks on-site, the cider develops a bubbly effervescence — a marriage between a bottle of beer and a glass of wine.

MCRITCHIE WINERY AND CIDERWORKS
315 Thurmond Post Office Road
Thurmond, NC 28683
(336) 874-3003

AUTUMN AT OZ

During Autumn at Oz, spot a cast of Wizard-seeking characters along the theme park's yellow-brick road.

D uring its annual Autumn at Oz event, Beech Mountain's historic Land of Oz theme park temporarily reopens to the public. Visit Auntie Em's farm, take a hayride, and skip down the yellow-brick road.

LAND OF OZ THEME PARK
2669 South Beech Mountain Parkway
Beech Mountain, NC 28604
(828) 387-2000
emeraldmtn.com

DRIVE THE PARKWAY

Grab your camera and cruise down some of our favorite mountain roads to take in the fall foliage. The Blue Ridge Parkway passes by dozens of popular natural attractions, like Mount Mitchell State Park and Linville Falls, but the road's overlooks offer spectacular vistas in their own right. Our recommendations: Waterrock Knob (MP 451.2) and Looking Glass Rock (MP 417). Give yourself a couple of hours of extra travel time so you can pull over along the parkway and enjoy the fresh air and fantastic views.

Our best fall advice: Travel higher, to where the roads start winding and the leaves are the first to change.

CRUISE LAKE TOXAWAY

When he opened the Greystone Inn, formerly the Toxaway Inn, Tim Lovelace learned that the owner took guests on a boat cruise. So he bought a six-passenger pontoon boat and named it *Miss Lucy Armstrong*, after the original owner's wife. The pontoon couldn't hold all of the guests, so Tim commissioned a large, wooden boat like the original one the Toxaway Inn had. Every evening, hotel guests board *Miss Lucy* to enjoy champagne; the fall foliage surrounding the lake; and stories of the inn, the lake, and Brevard.

**THE GREYSTONE INN
AT LAKE TOXAWAY**
Greystone Lane
Lake Toxaway, NC 28747
(800) 824-5766
laketoxaway.com

The *Miss Lucy* cruises Lake Toxaway, one of the many bodies of water to explore during autumn in Transylvania County.

WATCH LIKE A HAWK

Each fall, migrating bands of hawks, falcons, eagles, and ospreys soar through North Carolina. The hawks come on scimitar wings, coursing southward down the Blue Ridge. To the naked eye, the cloud of birds is a serene powder puff, but in 10X glass, it's a seething cauldron of vapor. Miles away and a mile high, the hawks wheel and gyre, like cinders from a fire, in a whirling formation known as a kettle. Then, suddenly, a lone hawk at the top peels out of the thermal like the stone in David's sling. Other birds follow, three and four at a time, rocketing southward down the ridge. To check out the action yourself, head for the High Country during early to mid-September through November. Pack a folding chair, binoculars, and a bird guide.

1. Bullhead Mountain
Just off the Blue Ridge Parkway near Sparta, this two-mile-long ridge offers great views to the northeast, east, and southeast.

2. Mahogany Rock Overlook
A Blue Ridge Parkway overlook at Milepost 235 in Alleghany County, this well-known raptor hotspot draws dozens of spectators per day. With huge views to the north and south, watchers spot kettles of hawks miles away.

3. Downtown Lenoir
Hawk enthusiasts gather in downtown Lenoir to bird-watch every fall. One year, volunteers counted more than 8,000 migrating hawks from this site.

Eastern red-tailed hawks frequent North Carolina, often staying for the winter months.

GREAT SMOKY MOUNTAINS RAILROAD

A century ago, the most effective way to get to our state's western hills was to ride the train. We don't need the railroad anymore, not for travel. But we do need it to reconnect with our past and our landscape. In the fall, the view from the railroad is all sugar maples, buttery poplars, and crimson oaks. A ride on the Great Smoky Mountains Railroad train starts at the depot in Bryson City, with at least two trip options every day: the Nantahala Gorge Excursion and the Tuckasegee River Excursion.

Just southwest of Bryson City, the train runs parallel to U.S. Highway 19, and through a mountain pasture.

GREAT SMOKY MOUNTAINS RAILROAD
226 Everett Street
Bryson City, NC 28713
(828) 586-8811
gsmr.com

COLFAX PERSIMMON FESTIVAL

I t grows right here in front of our noses. The dingy, orange-brown fruit doesn't shine under the fluorescent lights on grocery store aisles. Too many seeds, the fruit people say. Too perishable.

The persimmon is peculiar — and fleeting. Beginning as early as Labor Day, round globes the size of cherry tomatoes lose their grip on their spindly, sagging limbs. They tumble to the ground, suffering a bruise or two. Once they hit the ground, they last two days. That's it.

So we pack the mild, sweet flavor into puddings, pies, and cookies. These simple recipes, which populate the annual persimmon festival in Oak Ridge, are created using pantry staples (flour, sugar, butter), rendering desserts reminiscent of those found in country kitchens of long ago.

COLFAX PERSIMMON FESTIVAL
558 North Bunker Hill Road
Oak Ridge, NC 27310
(336) 682-5328
colfaxpersimmonfest.com

A persimmon on the branch may look ripe, but don't pick it. Wait on that jam until it's ready to fall.

Every October, the NC State Fair brings people from across the state together to celebrate our farms and farmers.

THE STATE FAIR

For 11 days at the North Carolina State Fair in Raleigh, we celebrate. We ride Ferris wheels, eat funnel cakes, and win prizes. But more important than what we do is the reason we do it. Since 1853, this fair has honored North Carolina agriculture. Behind those midway lights, farm families display their finest, from their best cows to their prettiest pumpkins. This October, take a ride, eat something sweet, and say thank you to the people who make the most of our land.

NC STATE FAIR
1025 Blue Ridge Road
Raleigh, NC 27607
(919) 733-2145
ncstatefair.org

STATESVILLE'S CAROLINA BALLOONFEST

On the third weekend in October, hot-air balloons rise above Statesville Regional Airport as part of the 42-year-old Carolina Balloon-Fest. Depending on the weather, the balloons will rise as high as 3,000 feet in the air and travel more than 15 miles — with you in it. Book a flight at the festival during one of two "mass ascensions," when as many as 50 hot-air balloons inflate and leave the ground simultaneously.

STATESVILLE REGIONAL AIRPORT
260 Hangar Drive
Statesville, NC 28625
carolinaballoonfest.com

Three thousand feet above Statesville, brave Carolina BalloonFest participants take to the sky.

Ross "BooBoo" Dalton, No. 50, excites race fans at Ace with his aggressive style and knack for winning.

FRIDAY NIGHT AT ACE SPEEDWAY

Ace Speedway's wooden grandstand fills with fans eager to watch their favorite drivers roar around the track. Wind from the cars rushes over the people, carrying the smell of warm rubber and car exhaust with it. After more than 50 years of playing host to fender-scraping stock-car races, this — the rush of adrenaline — still fills fans and drivers alike, keeping them coming back every Friday, all fall.

ACE SPEEDWAY
3401 Altamahaw Racetrack Road
Altamahaw, NC 27244
(336) 585-1200
acespeedway.com

Horses and hounds wait
in Southern Pines' Hobby
Field for The Blessing of
the Hounds hunt to begin.

THE BLESSING OF THE HOUNDS

Hunters and hounds gather reverently in Southern Pines on Thanksgiving Day before bursting across a field for the hunt. Wearing black and white vestments, the reverend begins the liturgy with Psalm 19:1, followed by The Lord's Prayer. She then raises her right hand high in the air and begins: *Bless, O Lord, we beseech You, rider and horse and hound ...*

The ecumenical tradition harkens back to early medieval days, when hunters believed an intercession from St. Hubert of Liège, the patron saint of hunters, would protect their hounds from disease and keep them safe during the hunt. But before the amen sounds, scores of tailgaters dress in their equestrian finest for a parade on the field.

MOORE COUNTY HOUNDS
1745 North May Street
Southern Pines, NC 28387
(910) 692-6889

AUTUMN LEAVES FESTIVAL

Years ago, this annual event in Mount Airy began as a celebration of the end of the tobacco and apple harvesting season. The tradition continues as more than 170 locals line the streets to demonstrate their talents and skills, which have been passed down through generations. Musicians pay tribute to the region's rich musical heritage — and so do the cooks: Civic and community groups serve classic Southern dishes, with hospitality.

AUTUMN LEAVES FESTIVAL
Downtown Mount Airy
(336) 786-6116
autumnleavesfestival.com

WARSAW VETERANS DAY PARADE

Duplin County residents are the keepers of a patriotic flame: America's oldest consecutive Veterans Day celebration. Street vendors, carnival games, a flyover, and free barbecue for men and women in uniform are all staples of a Warsaw Veterans Day. On Hill Street, gratitude for our country's veterans, and specifically for its North Carolinian sons and daughters, is palpable — especially at the parade's climax, when the grand marshal rides by in a convertible, marching bands behind.

Warsaw brings out the big guns for its annual Veterans Day parade, drawing thousands of patriotic visitors to Hill Street.

TOPSAIL SKATING RINK

School night roller-skating stays alive in a Topsail time capsule. From the outside, the white cinderblock building that holds Topsail Skating Rink doesn't look like much. Inside, the wooden floor is marked with scratches from years of skating. The office reveals rows of dusty skates and rusted suitcases filled with rollerblades kept here by once-regular customers, then left behind by necessity, college, or life beyond Topsail. In the daylight hours, the place is silent. But at night, starting at 7 p.m., the beat of the music fills the rink, along with the sound of wheels — so many wheels strapped to feet, flying across that old wooden floor.

TOPSAIL SKATING RINK
714 South Anderson Boulevard
Topsail Beach, NC 28445
(910) 328-2381

Muscadine or scuppernong? In shades of black to bronze, they're all muscadines. Scuppernong simply refers to the bronze variety.

MUSCADINE HERITAGE WINE TRAIL

Johnston County's Muscadine Heritage Wine Trail offers visitors a glimpse of North Carolina's muscadine winemaking traditions. The trail includes four stops: Adams Vineyards in Willow Spring, Enoch Winery in Benson, Gregory Vineyards in Angier, and Hinnant Family Vineyards in Pine Level. Each is family-owned (some since before the Revolutionary War), and all offer, in addition to musca-dine wine, food and traditional fruit wines. Start at any of the vineyards and take a tour of the fields and production facilities. After you've participated in a wine tasting, the vineyard will validate your Wine Trail stamp. Gather all four valida-tions in less than six months and receive a Muscadine Heritage Wine Trail T-shirt.

muscadineheritagewinetrail.com

NORTH CAROLINA YAM FESTIVAL

In 1995, North Carolina's General Assembly christened the sweet potato our state vegetable. They did so, reluctantly, at the urging of Celia Batchelor's fourth graders at Elvie Street School in Wilson, a resourceful collection of 10-year-olds who kept up a two-year campaign, earning themselves a nickname: The Tater Tots.

Today, at sweet potato harvesting time, Tabor City celebrates our state veggie with events including a cooking competition, fireman competition, yam auction, high school band competition, and a pageant. Live music and the festival parade pay equal tribute to honor our stellar spud.

NORTH CAROLINA YAM FESTIVAL
Downtown Tabor City
(910) 377-3012
ncyamfestival.com

CELEBRATE NATIONAL SEAFOOD MONTH

Carol Lohr and nine friends started the NC Seafood Festival in Morehead City in 1987 by each pitching in $100 to buy stationery. They met at a bar and drew the trademark logo of a fish wearing sunglasses on a cocktail napkin, and invited anyone who could come to enjoy an abundance of local seafood. Since then, this fall gathering has grown into the second-largest festival in the state. Nearly 100 food vendors offer their own interpretations of the ocean's bounty, from Down East clam chowder and shrimp burgers to calamari and marinated eel.

NC SEAFOOD FESTIVAL
Morehead City
Downtown waterfront
(252) 726-6273
ncseafoodfestival.org

OUR STATE'S HALLOWEEN HAUNTS

This October, follow our guide to North Carolina's best tricks and treats.

WESTERN

Jack-o'-lantern Pottery

John Dodson fires up his kiln at Mud Dabbers Pottery to make elaborate jack-o'-lanterns — a craft he learned from his father, who opened the pottery studio in 1988. Look for the lanterns' toothy grins on streets throughout Transylvania County.

MUD DABBERS POTTERY OF BREVARD
3623 Greenville Highway
Brevard, NC 28712
(828) 884-5131
muddabbers.com

Howl-O-Ween

The Western North Carolina Nature Center is home to more than 60 species of animals who, come October, "host" Halloween arts and crafts, costume contests, face painting — and bat ecology games.

WESTERN NORTH CAROLINA NATURE CENTER
72 Gashes Creek Road
Asheville, NC 28805
(828) 259-8092
wildwnc.org

CENTRAL

Aw Shucks Corn Maze

At Aw Shucks Corn Maze in Monroe, always expect the unexpected: Tireless visitors weave through corn mazes — which have a new design every year. If you make it out, sit by a bonfire for spooky stories and s'mores.

AW SHUCKS FARM
3718 Plyler Mill Road
Monroe, NC 28112
(704) 709-7000
awshuckscornmaze.com

Charlotte Haunted Bus Tour

Keep your seat on the tour bus, where it's safe. On this two-hour ride through the streets of Charlotte, listen to ghost stories based on each of the tour's stops. Participants are encouraged to bring a camera to capture the city's history — and maybe even paranormal activity.

CHARLOTTE GHOST TOURS
charlotteghosttours.com

Katie Compton leads the Walk by Lantern Light tour into Southport's eerie riverside graveyard.

EASTERN

Southport Ghost Tour
Ten years ago, in the middle of the night, a woman wandered alone through the streets of downtown Southport. Strolling past Civil War-era wrought-iron gates and looming oaks, Katie Compton gathered pieces of the town's history to create this spooky tour of Southport.

OLD SOUTH TOUR COMPANY
(910) 713-2072
oldsouthtourcompany.com

Scary Movies – Live
The Carolina Civic Center Historic Theater first opened in 1928 as a silent-film and vaudeville house. Today, the theater presents classic Halloween silent films paired with a live orchestra.

CAROLINA CIVIC CENTER HISTORIC THEATER
315 North Chestnut Street
Lumberton, NC 28358
(910) 738-4339
carolinaciviccenter.com

WINTER

Winter in North Carolina is all about attitude. Skiers and snow-lovers are wishin' and hopin'. Christmas folks have been decorating for weeks. If a polar plunge isn't your thing, now's the time to check out museums and galleries across the state, featuring everything from classic cars to Civil War artifacts, pottery to paintings. Settle down for a long winter's nap, or pull on your boots, button up, and cut your own Fraser fir. Don't just endure winter; embrace it!

In North Carolina, a snow day is a gift: an exquisite window view, a reason to play, and a pass to stay put.

HIT THE SLOPES

G roomed slopes, gorgeous vistas, and proximity to mountain towns like Boone and Blowing Rock make western North Carolina an ideal ski and snowboarding destination. On a weekend-long excursion, hit the slopes all day; shop and dine by night.

1. Sugar Mountain

In Avery County, about 17 miles southwest of Boone, Sugar Mountain maintains 21 slopes on 125 acres of skiable land. Seven lifts accommodate up to 8,800 people every hour during ski season, from November to March. For a good spot in the lift line, check in to The Highlands at Sugar, one- and two-bedroom lodging a short distance from the slopes.

SUGAR MOUNTAIN RESORT
(800) 784-2768
skisugar.com

2. Appalachian Ski Mountain

To maximize a one-day pass, head over to Appalachian Ski Mountain. All 12 slopes have lighting for night skiing, which means some skiers begin at 9 a.m., when the lifts open, and keep at it until 10 p.m., when they close. Plus, every Friday and Saturday night in January and February, the mountain holds a Midnight Blast, the only late-night skiing in the High Country.

APPALACHIAN SKI MOUNTAIN
(828) 295-7828
appskimtn.com

76

When you stand atop one of Sugar Mountain's 21 slopes, just think: It's all downhill from here.

3. Beech Mountain

At 5,506 feet above sea level, Beech Mountain is the highest ski mountain on the Eastern Seaboard. In addition to 15 trails and eight ski lifts (including the only high-speed quad lift in the state), Beech also has two terrain parks and an ice-skating rink, open from November to March. Consider nearby Archer's Mountain Inn for a hotel room, cabin rental, bar, or restaurant.

BEECH MOUNTAIN RESORT
(800) 438-2093
beechmountainresort.com

NATIONAL GINGERBREAD HOUSE COMPETITION

The rules at the National Gingerbread House Competition in Asheville may be strict (the main structure must be at least 75 percent gingerbread), but this annual event continues to be a whimsical treat for both competitors and observers. Food artists from all over the country come to Asheville to have their work judged for overall appearance, originality and creativity, difficulty, precision, and consistency of theme. Post-judging, the houses remain on display at the Omni Grove Park Inn through the first of the new year.

OMNI GROVE PARK INN
290 Macon Avenue
Asheville, NC 28804
(828) 252-2711
omnihotels.com

THE LIGHTS OF McADENVILLE

Driving the 1.3 miles through McAdenville can take hours in December, but the cars line up anyway to behold the spectacle that is Christmas Town U.S.A. Some longtime residents say the birth of Christmas Town U.S.A. happened in 1956, when the McAdenville Men's Club used lights to decorate some trees around the community center. Others claim that the first case of exterior illumination was a solo effort in front of McAdenville Methodist Church: When a would-be Grinch stole the lights, a generous offer by William J. Pharr, owner of the local textile mill, to replace them led to the sprouting of lights all around town. Still others insist that the original tree motif, the pattern that all others have been modeled after, actually debuted in front of the headquarters of the mill before 1956. But no matter which origin story one believes, the draw of the town's glow is indisputable: Almost 1,000 times as many people as McAdenville has residents descend upon this town from as far away as England every December to gaze at some 450,000 lights.

A half-century ago, the little town of McAdenville earned its place in the Christmas spotlight.

THE CHERRYVILLE NEW YEAR'S SHOOTERS

Cover your ears and stand back. Beginning at the stroke of midnight on New Year's Day, the Cherryville New Year's Shooters blast in the new year with a tradition observed in North Carolina for more than 200 years. Using muskets filled with black powder (no bullets, we promise), the gun-bearers march around town, firing their guns every hour, on the hour, throughout the morning, and chanting good tidings for the coming year.

CHERRYVILLE NEW YEAR'S SHOOTERS
(704) 435-3061
cherryvilleshooters.com

BILTMORE CHRISTMAS

Biltmore was born on Christmas Eve. George Vanderbilt introduced his grand home to family and friends on December 24, 1895. In the years that followed, the Vanderbilts left behind many more stories of life inside the walls of North Carolina's most famous home. At Christmas, take the regular Biltmore tour, but know that this is the estate at its finest: a tree at every turn, hundreds of wreaths, thousands of ornaments, boughs and bows winding down the grand staircase. Every light strand, every magical detail, handled with care.

BILTMORE ESTATE
One Lodge Street
Asheville, NC 28803
(800) 411-3812
biltmore.com

Biltmore shines during winter nights for the duration of the Christmas season.

SANTA CLIMBS CHIMNEY ROCK

How is Santa able to climb down millions of chimneys around the world in a single night? He practices. In the days leading up to Christmas, he'll be climbing one of the world's largest chimneys with 200-foot rappels at Chimney Rock State Park. (Also, he may take a break at the mall.)

CHIMNEY ROCK STATE PARK
(800) 277-9611
chimneyrockpark.com

FOLK SCHOOL CHRISTMAS CRAFT MARKET

In 1925, in a remote corner of southwestern North Carolina, far from the glittering lights of Asheville, a woman sang. She sang while walking through the meadows of Brasstown. She sang while delivering eggs to her neighbors. She sang for her friends, the soft notes of her soprano voice wrapping around them like a blanket. The woman, Olive Dame Campbell, wrote down

Each year, locals arrive in Brasstown to help make decorations for the John C. Campbell Folk School's campus.

the ballads of Appalachian folk songs. The collection brought her fame, but it wasn't the ballads that sustained her legacy in North Carolina. It was her love of the people here, a love so strong that she founded a school in 1925 to help them learn to market their skills. She named it after her late husband, John C. Campbell. Today, Olive's voice is preserved at the John C. Campbell Folk School, where, for a special seven days each year, Holiday in the Mountains Week takes place. This week of classes gives you the opportunity to learn to craft your own gifts for loved ones this holiday season.

JOHN C. CAMPBELL FOLK SCHOOL
1 Folk School Road
Brasstown, NC 28902
(828) 837-2775

Beeswax candles and carols, sweet buns and coffee: the savored elements of Wake Forest University's lovefeast.

MORAVIAN LOVEFEAST

Pass a warm, creamy coffee and a sweet bun along, and for a moment, the stranger beside you becomes kin. The best part of lovefeast, a traditional Christmas service brought to North Carolina from Europe by the Moravians in 1753, comes when hundreds of raised hands illuminate the darkness with the light of beeswax candles. Celebrate lovefeast in Winston-Salem, which was founded by Moravians.

St. Philips Moravian Church
913 South Church Street
(336) 770-5933

Wait Chapel
Wake Forest University
Reynolda Campus
Winston-Salem, NC 27109
(336) 758-5210

THE NUTCRACKER

Each ballerina's step is prescribed by those who've taken them before, and each dance is a part of the history of this classic holiday tradition, performed each year by our state's dance companies. For those whose Christmas season isn't complete without the story of Clara, the Nutcracker Prince, and the Sugarplum Fairy — or Tchaikovsky's beloved score — look out for these annual performances of *The Nutcracker*.

Carolina Ballet
Chapel Hill, Durham, Raleigh
(919) 719-0900
carolinaballet.com

University of North Carolina School of the Arts
Winston-Salem
(336) 770-3399
uncsa.edu

Walkerdance Ballet Theatre
Burlington
(336) 214-3296
thewalkerdance.com

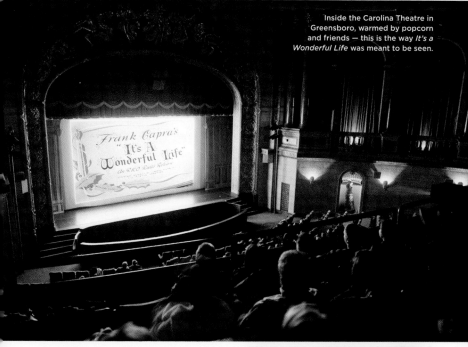

Inside the Carolina Theatre in Greensboro, warmed by popcorn and friends — this is the way *It's a Wonderful Life* was meant to be seen.

CHRISTMAS MOVIE CLASSICS AT THE CAROLINA THEATRE

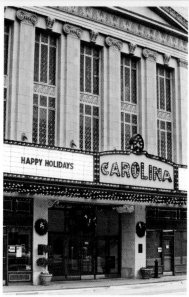

The Carolina Theatre gets in the holiday spirit with its Carolina Classic Movie series, bringing to the big screen gems such as *It's a Wonderful Life*, *A Christmas Story*, *Holiday Inn*, *White Christmas*, *National Lampoon's Christmas Vacation*, and *Elf*. Join fellow movie lovers as they rejoice in the season with screen families and characters that we welcomed into our hearts and homes long ago.

CAROLINA THEATRE
310 South Greene Street
Greensboro, NC 27401
(336) 333-2605
carolinatheatre.com

MITCHELL'S NURSERY POINSETTIAS

A poinsettia's life has three stages. The plant that decorates your Christmas table starts in a place far from North Carolina, like New Jersey or California. As a tiny cutting from a parent plant, it takes a ride in a refrigerated truck. The truck takes the poinsettia to Mitchell's Nursery & Greenhouse in King, where it begins its second stage. Gardeners transplant it into a bigger pot, eight inches, or maybe 10, with lots of potting soil and room to grow. It receives fertilizer and water, and goes through growing pains when gardeners pinch its top.

The gardeners dress it up with shiny green foil and a red ribbon, and in December, it isn't about the plant anymore. The grown-up poinsettia now lives to give joy to others — that's its reward.

Jim and Judy Mitchell, the owners of Mitchell's Nursery, know that poinsettia journey well. They're the gardeners who care for these traditional Christmas plants in the crucial middle stage. Mitchell's Nursery offers 90 varieties of poinsettias for sale every year — some so new they have yet to be named.

MITCHELL'S NURSERY & GREENHOUSE
1088 West Dalton Road
King, NC 27021
(336) 983-4107
mnandg.com

WINTER FARMERS MARKETS

North Carolina is one of the highest-ranked states for its number of winter farmers markets. Find out what makes these four Piedmont winter markets worth a visit.

1. Greensboro Farmers Curb Market

With roots that reach back to 1874, this farmers market is one of the oldest in the state. We suspect that artisanal breads and goat cheese spreads weren't such hot commodities back then, but they're two good reasons to shop here this winter.

501 Yanceyville Street
Greensboro, NC 27405
Saturdays, January-March
7 a.m.-noon

2. Matthews Community Farmers Market

The comforts of this town's outdoor farmers market may take the edge off the morning chill. Despite having to rise early, on Saturdays in downtown Matthews you can shop for hardy greens, root vegetables, fresh eggs, and honey.

188 North Trade Street
Matthews, NC 28105
Saturdays, December-March
8-10 a.m.

3. Atherton Mill and Market

Charlotteans like new things, and this farmers market is no exception. It opened in 2010 in one of the city's fastest-growing neighborhoods, South End. The urban market offers produce, baked goods, crafts, and coffee.

2140 South Boulevard
Charlotte, NC 28203
Tuesdays, 10 a.m.-7 p.m.
Wednesday-Friday, 10 a.m.-2 p.m.
Saturdays, 9 a.m.-2 p.m.

4. Durham Farmers Market

Durham's culinary gurus stock their kitchens with goods from this market. While shopping here may not make you Ashley Christensen, if you attend a cooking demonstration, your collard greens may taste better.

501 Foster Street
Durham, NC 27701
Saturdays, December-March
10 a.m.-noon

The International Civil Rights Center & Museum is located in the same building where the Greensboro Four took a stand.

THE CIVIL RIGHTS CENTER & MUSEUM

When Franklin McCain, Ezell Blair Jr., Joseph McNeil, and David Richmond walked into F.W. Woolworth's in Greensboro on February 1, 1960, and sat down at the "whites-only" lunch counter, they knew they were doing more than ordering lunch. The young black men, students at North Carolina Agricultural and Technical State University, took a stand against segregation and began their protest. The next day, they returned with more than 20 students. By the third day, more than 300 joined them; soon 1,000 marched to the store. Six months later, Woolworth's relented and ended segregation at their lunch counters across the country. Now known as the Greensboro Four, McCain, Blair, McNeil, and Richmond helped launch the sit-in movement that swept across the South and marked another step toward equality. Their actions are memorialized at the International Civil Rights Center & Museum, an ideal educational outing to remedy winter cabin fever.

INTERNATIONAL CIVIL RIGHTS CENTER & MUSEUM
134 South Elm Street
Greensboro, NC 27401
(336) 274-9199
sitinmovement.org

MEET A FURRY FORECASTER

We find ourselves in one hopeful moment, gripping the edge of our seats, crossing our fingers behind our backs, breath held, waiting for the verdict: Will he see it? Will winter's chill nip us for six more weeks? At the Museum of Natural Sciences' Groundhog Day celebration in Raleigh, Sir Walter Wally predicts what the rest of February and March hold for North Carolinians. Still, his fellow furry forecasters — Queen Charlotte and Carolina Chuck — may beg to differ.

GROUNDHOG DAY CELEBRATION
NC Museum of Natural Sciences
11 West Jones Street
Raleigh, NC 27601
(919) 707-9800
naturalsciences.org

Groundhog Sir Walter Wally doesn't mind handler Dee Freeman's spotlight — unless it comes with a shadow.

CAROLINA HURRICANES HOCKEY

Hurricane season is just getting started in Raleigh, home to the NHL's Carolina Hurricanes. "Caniacs," as fans are known, show up to PNC Arena to tailgate hours before the puck drops, and to share theories on what the 'Canes need to do to win another Stanley Cup — like they did when they won in 2006. Come game time, the team's mascot, Stormy the ice hog, leads the players onto the ice waving a giant hurricane warning flag — so opponents can't say they weren't warned.

hurricanes.nhl.com

CAROLINA CHOCOLATE FESTIVAL

Not only is the Carolina Chocolate Festival a chance to partake in some of the most delectable of our state's sweets, it's also an opportunity to give back. This annual charity event gathers vendors from North Carolina and beyond inside the Crystal Coast Civic Center in Morehead City to offer everything from chocolate cakes to tortes to ice cream. Event favorites include taste testings, the Chocolate Spa, and the 5K Cocoa Run. Chocolate lovers, unite.

CAROLINA CHOCOLATE FESTIVAL
(252) 393-2011
carolinachocolatefestival.com

Boaters and spectators gather at Wrightsville Beach for the annual North Carolina Holiday Flotilla.

HOLIDAY FLOTILLA

No parade has seen such grace as when fishing boats and pleasure crafts deck their decks and cruise the Intracoastal Waterway. See them electrify our eastern waterfronts at one of these holiday flotillas.

1. Beaufort
Crystal Coast Christmas Flotilla
(252) 728-1638
maritimefriends.org

2. Carolina Beach
Island of Lights Holiday Flotilla
(910) 458-5507
pleasureislandoflights.com

3. Southport
Southport Christmas Flotilla
(910) 454-4327
downtownsouthport.org

4. Wrightsville Beach
North Carolina Holiday Flotilla
(910) 256-2120
ncholidayflotilla.org

In New Bern, Jonkonnu communicates a timeless language of hope.

NEW BERN JONKONNU CHRISTMAS

"Jonkonnu is coming! Jonkonnu is coming!" a woman shouts to the crowd gathered for New Bern's annual Christmas Candlelight event at Tryon Palace. A man in a three-piece suit and top hat steps up and explains: For one day every winter — when the chores were done, the summer's harvest stored, and the land prepared for planting in the spring — his enslaved ancestors were allowed to dance and sing through the streets. They called the celebration Jonkonnu.

Simon Spalding, a former manager of Tryon Palace's living-history programs, recreated the tradition here around 2000. He wanted the Christmas celebration to reflect the entire population of Colonial New Bern, which was about half African-American. New Bern remains one of the few places where you can still experience Jonkonnu. For an hour, people of all colors come together and dance, the way their ancestors always dreamed.

TRYON PALACE
529 South Front Street
New Bern, NC 28562
(800) 767-1560
tryonpalace.org

The Dolphin Dip's most determined and uninhibited participants are the first to reach Surf City's chilly waters.

BRAVE A POLAR PLUNGE

The draw of the Surf City Dolphin Dip is partly Brian Moxey's power of persuasion. Partly that, and partly the renewed energies that come from crossing the threshold into a fresh year. That's why more than 5,000 people run into 40-degree water on New Year's Day. It's a little bit crazy, and like most crazy things, America's largest New Year's Day swim event began with a dare.

On New Year's Eve 2002, Moxey challenged a group of his friends: At noon tomorrow, he told them, we plunge. They did. Word got around, and the next year, 120 people showed up. Attendees brought friends. Their friends brought friends, and the craze keeps growing.

After a countdown, the eager, huddled mass of people — many in outlandish costumes — bursts into a mad dash, splashing recklessly into the ocean. The squealing, yelling, and bellowing announce: The beginning of this year hasn't just washed over us. We've willingly, enthusiastically, overcome its first challenge.

For information on the next year's Dolphin Dip, visit dolphindip.net.

NORTH CAROLINA JAZZ FESTIVAL

In 1980, local dermatologist Dr. Harry VanVelsor's love of jazz convinced Wilmington to host its very own festival dedicated to the genre. Since then, famed artists from America and abroad have made the Wilmington Hilton Riverside their destination for one weekend each February, and bring world-class jazz to a longtime, dedicated North Carolina audience. The weekend festival showcases different jazz styles to appeal to audiences' broad range of tastes.

NORTH CAROLINA JAZZ FESTIVAL
(910) 793-1111
ncjazzfestival.com

ORIENTAL'S NEW YEAR'S DRAGON

When one New Year just isn't enough, ring it in twice. For more than 30 years, Oriental has commemorated the Chinese Lunar New Year with the Running of the Dragon on New Year's Eve. This massive dragon (powered by 40 or 50 pairs of feet), and its smoke-snorting head, appears beside the harbor with the sound of bells, drums, horns, noisemakers, and shouts of "Happy New Year!" Crowd members will have two opportunities during the event to pursue, reach, and touch the dragon's tail for a year's worth of good luck.

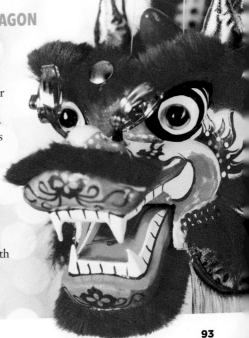

DOWNTOWN ORIENTAL
(252) 249-0555
townoforiental.com

CHOOSE AND CUT YOUR CHRISTMAS TREE

The smell of pine permeating the room. The brush of needles as you place presents on soft red velvet. There's something special about a tree you picked out yourself — and something even more special when it comes with a memory of visiting a local tree farm. Here are our recommendations for where to choose and cut the perfect North Carolina Christmas tree.

WESTERN

BROWN'S CHOOSE & CUT
2648 NC Highway 194 North
Boone, NC 28607
(828) 264-2800

JONAS RIDGE TREE FARM
8040 Joe Poore Road
Jonas Ridge, NC 28641
(828) 733-4654
jonasridgetreefarm.com

**FIR HEAVEN SAKE
CHRISTMAS TREE FARM**
40 Fir Heaven Sake Lane
Topton, NC 28781
(828) 361-4878
ncchristmastrees.com

CENTRAL

BROCK'S TREE FARM
8317 Lawdraker Road
Apex, NC 27539
(919) 333-6696
ncfarmfresh.com

**NORTHLAKE CHRISTMAS
TREES & NURSERY**
7326 Meadowbrook Road
Benson, NC 27504
(919) 894-3524
northlakechristmastreenursery.com

R FRESH FIRS
571 Daisy Thompson Road
Roxboro, NC 27574
(336) 322-3031
daisyhilltopfarm.com

EASTERN

**BEAUTANCUS
CHRISTMAS TREE FARM**
1569 Beautancus Road
Mount Olive, NC 28365
(919) 778-7060

WILSON'S TREE FARM
County Home Road
Winterville, NC 28590
(910) 296-0824
wilsonstreefarmnc.com

JUSTICE FARMS
1325 Gould Road
Jacksonville, NC 28540
(910) 346-6783
justicefarms.com

For many families, hunting for the perfect Christmas tree on a farm like R Fresh Firs in Roxboro is a tradition that begins in childhood and gets passed down through generations.

GEOFF WOOD

TO ORDER MORE

If you've enjoyed *A Four-Season Guide to North Carolina*, think of all your family, friends, and coworkers who would enjoy it, too!

CALL THE OUR STATE STORE

AT

(800) 948-1409

OR VISIT

OURSTATESTORE.COM

Our State